ideals®
CHRISTMAS

D0580228

Dedicated to a celebration—through poetry and prose—of the American ideals of faith in God, loyalty to country, and love of family.

And all the bells on earth did ring
For joy—our Saviour Christ was born
On Christmas Day.
—Author Unknown

IDEALS—Vol. 61, No. 6, November 2004 IDEALS (ISSN 0019-137X, USPS 256-240) is published six times a year: January, March, May, July, September, and November by IDEALS PUBLICATIONS, a division of Guideposts, 39 Seminary Hill Road, Carmel, NY 10512. Copyright © 2004 by IDEALS PUBLICATIONS, a division of Guideposts. All rights reserved. The cover and entire contents of IDEALS are fully protected by copyright and must not be reproduced in any manner whatsoever. Title IDEALS registered U.S. Patent Office. Printed and bound in the USA. Printed on Weyerhaeuser Husky. The paper used in this publication meets the minimum requirements of American National Standard for Information Sciences—Permanence of Paper for Printed Library Materials, ANSI Z39.48-1984. Periodicals postage paid at Carmel, New York, and additional mailing offices. Canadian mailed under Publications Mail Agreement Number 40010140. POSTMASTER: Send address changes to Ideals, 39 Seminary Hill Road, Carmel, NY 10512. CANADA POST: Send address changes to Guideposts PO Box 1051, Fort Erie ON L2A 6C7. For subscription or customer service questions, contact Ideals Publications, a division of Guideposts, 39 Seminary Hill Road, Carmel, NY 10512. Fax 845-228-2115. Reader Preference Service: We occasionally make our mailing lists available to other companies whose products or services might interest you. If you prefer not to be included, please write to Ideals Customer Service.

ISBN 0-8249-1235-7 GST 893989236

Visit the *Ideals* website at www.idealsbooks.com

Cover: Brilliant red poinsettias from Marion County, Oregon, add traditional bright color to holiday celebrations. Photograph by Steve Terrill.

Inside front cover: A lovely young lady has prepared a special Christmas basket in this painting by Norman Prescott Davies, entitled CHRISTMAS FARE. *Image provided by Fine Art Photographic Library, Ltd., London/Courtesy N. R. Omell Gallery, London.*

Inside back cover: A Merry Christmas! A nineteenth-century card by an unknown artist wishes everyone the best of the season. Image provided by Fine Art Photographic Library, Ltd., London.

In This Issue

Red firs are blanketed with snow near Bull Gap in Rogue River National Forest, Jackson County, Oregon. Photograph by Steve Terrill.

Overleaf: A winter storm clears over Queens Garden and Boat Mesa in Bryce Canyon National Park, Utah. Photograph by Terry Donnelly/Donnelly Austin Photography.

Wonderful Wintertime

Nora M. Bozeman

Beneath a sky of cobalt blue,
The day is wrapped in winter's hue.
Diamond-sparkled snowflakes fly,
Like frost-kissed magic from on high.

Vivid blue jays, brave and bold,
Hop around and loudly scold.

Cardinals decorate the scene,
On snowy boughs of evergreen.

Icy winds sculpt drifts of white
And etch each silver-frosted night.
December hangs her frozen head
And sleeps upon an ermine bed.

The Lacemaker

Del Turner

In the middle of the night, she came
To weave a pattern on my window pane.
With delicate strands of crystal thread,
She looped and stitched; we slept in bed.
With swirls and scallops, she adorned each space
In the finest beauty of winter lace.

READERS' REFLECTIONS

Readers are invited to submit original poetry for possible publication in future issues of IDEALS. *Please send typed copies only; manuscripts will not be returned. Writers receive payment for each published submission. Send material to Readers' Reflections, Ideals Publications, 535 Metroplex Drive, Suite 250, Nashville, Tennessee 37211.*

Snow World
Raymond Bottom
Monroe, Michigan

The world is covered with fairyland paint
Of the purest, dazzling white,
By sly Jack Frost with his whitewash brush,
Who silently worked last night.

The green firs and pines have lacy white frocks;
Aspens wear mittens of white;

The breathless beauty of snow-covered peaks
Reflects the dawn's changing lights.

All the world seems pure, serene
In the wonder of the snow.
Only the youngsters break the quiet;
The elders dream of long ago.

Winter
Debi Lankford
Fairfield, Iowa

Crisp and clear
　　the air tonight—
Silent, still,
　　and crystal white.

Snowflakes dancing
　　all around,
Drifting softly
　　to the ground,

Like a whisper
　　barely heard,
Sweet and gentle
　　as a bird.

In every breath,
　　with every sigh,
Winter paints
　　as she walks by.

First Snowfall
Linda Elizabeth Ironside
London, Ontario

Angel feathers
fill the sky,
fluttering down
from heaven on high,
sprinkling the trees
and each upturned face;

they dance through the air
with celestial grace,
settling so softly
on rooftops below—
the magic descent
of winter's first snow.

Winter's Sleep
Jeanne M. Wilkes
Bountiful, Utah

Heavy with slumber,
Winter readies her downy bed,
Spreading a fleecy white blanket
Over mountains, trees,
And frozen streams.
She draws her lace curtain
Across the skies
And lies down to icicle dreams.

Indigo Eve
Laurie L. LaMontagne
Hampton Falls, New Hampshire

The sky's a shade of indigo,
The moon, a paler blue.
Stars shimmer with a silver glow,
For evening clouds are few.
While gazing at this darkened sky,
I watch an owl's arrow flight
Add a touch of simple beauty
To this quiet winter night.

7

My Son's First Snow

Harry E. Ezell

Pressed against the windowpane,
My baby watches his first snow
With eyes and mouth in wonder wide
At sight of this strange countryside,
All white beneath the sparkling tide
Of freshly falling snow.

Ah, Son, the storms of life with pain
May scar your face and heart, I know;
But may they never from your eyes
Remove the light that in them lies,
As now, in wondering surprise,
You watch the falling snow.

Winters Past

Mary Catherine Johnson

I remember long, long icicles that glittered in the sun,
Like crystals flashing from the eaves of houses, every one!
First stretching longer, day by day,
Then dripping, shrinking, the array
Of sparkling spears a-dangle disappeared, and there were none.

I remember frosty forest ferns upon the window glass,
Those early morning etchings as of jungle leaf and grass,
Which wavered with alarm
And vanished as the air grew warm,
But overnight appeared again with glorious foliage mass.

I remember tall brick chimneys on rooftops everywhere,
And noses pinched by acrid smell of coal smoke in the air,
And watching grimy soot-fall fly
Onto the laundry hung to dry—
And laughing, sliding on the snow as grownups turned to stare.

This tranquil winter scene on a farm recalls the slower pace of old-fashioned holidays. Photograph by Larry LeFever/Grant Heilman.

NO TWO MOMENTS ARE ANY MORE ALIKE
THAN TWO SNOWFLAKES.

—ZORA NEALE HURSTON

SLICE OF LIFE
Edna Jaques

SNOWSTORM

The cars go by on softly muted wheels;
    The houses have a homemade country look;
The Church of the Redeemer, there on Bloor,
    Looks like a picture from an ancient book.
The roofs are thatches, with furry layers of snow
    Tacked on like batting at a Christmas show.

White-haloed lampposts stand like sentinels
    Before the sleeping castle of their lord;
A million wires furred with downy white
    Glisten and sparkle like a Christmas cord.
The whole town has a happy, festive air,
    Gay as the dancing at a country fair.

A little boy pulls a scarlet sleigh,
    A lady picks out her way to church,
A bird half-hidden in the shrubbery
    Finds his balance on a snowy perch;
The house across the street changed in the night
    Into a fairy palace—shining, white.

Just for a day, let us be young again,
    And let this gentle peace be truly ours:
The snowy paths, the little gates ajar,
    The quaint, top-heavy look of laden towers,
A city wrapped in cellophane and wool—
    God's Christmas package, strangely beautiful.

Country Winter Fun

Ralph W. Seager

There's a big difference between a country winter and a city one. Out there, winter makes the country over; in the city it is winter that is made over. For young ones, the country winter is wonderful. The white clouds, which formed such fantastic scenes in the summer skies, have come down to earth for the sake of small children. As the sky comes drifting in under our feet, we become unbound from earth, climbing heavenward on snow-fashioned staircases to watching us at our snug play in the evening. It is a confirmation of the belief that we can know life in this separation from our ordinary footmarks; that walking upon the water can be an act of truth as well as a symbolic one; that where no flower is possible, there will be flowers. This is winter in the country.

It was a good thing that we had barrels in those days instead of the modern steel drums. How else could we have gone sailing down the hardened slopes of winter? Solid

There · is · no · other · time · of · the · year · when · the sky · comes · between · us · and · the · earth.

go sailing on this whiteness as cousins to the wind. We are the chief participants in weather's detached and fanciful riot of fun. There is no other time of the year when the sky comes between us and the earth. It stays while we walk upon it.

Winter is the white phenomenon. Not only do clouds come down as cushions under our feet, but the very waters stand still and let us walk upon them. Trees that are unleafed and stark against the alabaster scene suddenly flower with crystal blossoms, more elegant, more scintillating than any others they may have later. Frost, ferny and crystalline, presses its face to the window, oak staves were our need, and how my sister and I begged for Dad to declare one of the barrels in the barn as ours. It is not the easiest work in the world to persuade a staunch barrel to give up its shape, to let loose of its hoops and wire, to collapse in a heap. But we had the resources of desire on our side. We must fly on the great clouds.

The outside bend of the stave was worked over with sandpaper, scraped with pieces of broken glass until hand-smooth, then rubbed thoroughly with paraffin. Next, a toe strap was nailed across the width of the stave. Fastening that toe strap was the critical point of the entire operation. Putting a nail into the narrowness of that hard core oak without splitting it required patience, persistence, and a small thumb.

Our winter footwear consisted of high, four-buckle arctics. With these we wore long, black leggings. There must have been a dozen buttons on either side of these leggings, and the buttonholes were always wearing too big. By the time the top button was in its place, the first one had popped out. Sweaters, coats, and mufflers smothered us nose-deep. Our mittens were tethered to each other by a string that ran up one sleeve, around the neck, and back down through the other sleeve. Stocking caps were pulled down over ears. It was impossible to fall down and get hurt. The problem really was, could you get up again?

The staves were heavy, cumbersome, and curved like a chair rocker. It was like riding downhill with a rocking horse under each foot. Off we would go, my sister and I, with these awkward wings on our feet.

At the top of the drift we looked down across the icy polish of the field, turned our stave-skis in a straight-ahead direction, and shoved off. It was a teetering, tongue-biting ride. We were seldom perpendicular. A successful descent was a triumph.

A snowfall offers a wonderful opportunity for outdoor winter play, as portrayed in this nineteenth-century Christmas card by an unknown artist, entitled BONNE ANNEE. Image provided by Fine Art Photographic Library, Ltd., London.

Then back up for another try.

Barrel staves, oaken wings, red-cheeked cherubim sliding on frozen clouds, fire in our faces, chilblain on our toes, laughter, and love—everything was there in my country winter.

Blue Boy

Shirley Sallay

I had a sled that Grandpa made;
It meant the world to me,
With wooden bed and runners,
A beauty for all to see.

I pulled it to the top of a hill
When the snow was soft and new,
'Twas the envy of all my friends,
With its bold new coat of blue.

How many hours of winter
Did I spend upon that sled,
Bundled warm in my snowsuit
With a scarf upon my head?

When I see the sleds of my children,
Streamlined, with metal bright,
I dream again of "Blue Boy"
And that snowy hill, with delight.

I know they'd call it old-fashioned,
But if I had it once more, here,
I'd race them down the hill again
And win, with a mighty cheer.

Many like the new ones,
With varnished wood and chrome,
But give me my old "Blue Boy"
And snow on the hill back home.

Antique sleds are displayed on a log cabin wall with other vintage winter equipment. Photograph by Jessie Walker.

Iowa Sled Ride

Marian Fulton Daggett

Papa forked sweet-smelling hay in the sled,
Then in their stout harness our horses he led.
Soon hitched securely, they stomped in
        the snow.
"Come on," called Papa, "A-sledding
        we'll go."

Hatted and coated and booted and muffed,
We clambered in wildly; the hay was
        all roughed.
With blankets and lap robes we all tried
        our best
To make for ourselves a warm little nest.

Away! Now the sled was all rapture
        and noise,
Filled with five giggly girls and five
        wiggly boys,
Slipping so smoothly along in the snow—
Over the white countryside we did go.

Over a hill, down a clean, frosty road,
The horses seemed happy to carry their load.
The songs that we sang and the stories
        we told
Echoed in air that was still from the cold.

Now joyous and free to adventuring go,
We have a father to guide us above the
        deep snow,
And know, that no matter how far we
        may roam,
He will take us all safely and
        happily home.

BITS & PIECES

I'm dreaming of a white Christmas,
Just like the ones I used to know. . . .
—*Irving Berlin*

*W*inter comes to rule the varied year.
—*James Thomson*

*T*he splendor of silence—of snow-jeweled hills and of ice.
—*Ingram Crockett*

*I*t is the sea that whitens the roof.
The sea drifts through the winter air.
It is the sea that the north wind makes.
The sea is in the falling snow.
—*Wallace Stevens*

*R*ound and round, like a dance of snow
In a dazzling drift . . .
—*Robert Browning*

*S*now, snow over the whole
land across all boundaries.
—*Boris Pasternak*

16

At Christmas I no more desire a rose
Than wish a snow in May's newfangled shows,
But like of each thing that in season grows.
—*William Shakespeare*

Christmas is here:
Winds whistle shrill,
Icy and chill.
Little care we;
Little we fear
Weather without,
Shelter'd about
The Mahogany Tree.
—*William Makepeace Thackeray*

And when a snowflake finds a tree,
"Good-day!" it says,"Good-day to thee!
Thou art so bare and lonely, dear,
I'll rest and call my comrades here."
—*Mary Mapes Dodge*

I have forgotten much, but still remember
The poinsettia's red . . .
—*Claude McKay*

Christmas Valley

Elizabeth Swain Lawson

I stand on a hill, looking downward
To the snowy valley below;
I see smoke spirals from chimneys
And windows with candles' warm glow.

Children skate on a shallow pond,
Within the churchyard's domain,
And men ride upon wood-piled sleds
With Old Dobbin pulling the reins.

As I scan the slope nearest me,
Youths are merrily bobsledding,
And little creatures of the wood
Deep in their nests are bedding.

And I feel a sweet awareness
Of a Presence from above,
Whose birth in lowly Bethlehem
Filled all the world with love.

I pick up my little fir tree
Because twilight is drawing near
And wend home down a snowy path
For the happiest time of year.

*This small, snow-covered valley in East Orange, Vermont,
welcomes visitors. Photograph by William H. Johnson.*

Simple Joys

Sandi Keaton-Wilson

A cedar bough,
A candle lit,
A rocking chair
In which to sit,

A glowing hearth,
A loving smile,
Companionship
To pass the while,

An open book,
A kitten's purr,
Simmering pot
To sniff and stir,

A baby's laugh,
A grandma's tale,

A dust of snow
On front-porch rail,

A whispered prayer,
A whistled carol,
A biting wind
And warm apparel,

A childhood game,
A lifelong friend,
A cheerful card
To sign and send—

These simple joys
Are much the reason
For celebrating
The Christmas season.

Coming Home

Lois J. Martinec

The fine-line script of chimney smoke
Writes "Welcome" in the sky.
This country road brings memories
As miles go skimming by.
There are thoughts of gentle living,
Of scenes from Christmas past,
Of sounds so warm and homey,
Where roots hold deep and fast.
What bonds of love bind and keep,
Time and distance cannot separate.
I'm coming home; it's Christmas,
Where loved ones live and wait.

*The happy welcome for family returning home for Christmas
is depicted in this painting by Bob Pettes, entitled MEETING
THE TRAIN. Copyright © Bob Pettes. All rights reserved.*

THEODORE ROOSEVELT

When Theodore Roosevelt Sr. and his wife, Martha Bulloch Roosevelt, welcomed their second child on October 27, 1858, they had high hopes for their son. Beginning at age three, however, the boy was plagued by severe asthma and he remained small and weak. In 1870, a concerned Theodore Roosevelt Sr. approached his twelve-year-old son and told the boy that through hard work he must make his body as strong as his mind. At that moment, the young boy resolved to overcome his challenges and prove himself to both his father and the world. Surely his parents could not have guessed that their once-sickly child would plunge into life with an unstoppable spirit and become the powerful and well-loved Theodore Roosevelt.

Raised with a large, loving family and the privileges of the aristocratic class, young Teddy Roosevelt did nothing halfway. Each day he improved himself by lifting weights, boxing, hunting, and indulging his passion for reading and nature. When he left for Harvard in 1876, his family expected him to become a naturalist. But after graduation, Roosevelt became involved in the seedy world of local Republican politics. There the bespectacled Roosevelt, with his boundless energy, toothy grin, and unapologetic manner, found his calling. He was elected as an assemblyman in 1881 and spent three terms trying to right wrongs the way his father had taught him. Yet he was still faced with personal challenges. His health failed him at times; and his first wife, Alice, died unexpectedly after giving birth to their first child and just hours after typhoid fever caused his mother's death. A distraught Roosevelt left political life and escaped west to the Dakota Badlands, where he spent two years as a cattle rancher.

Although adventure and the great outdoors would always beckon him, Roosevelt's future was back East. He married a childhood friend, Edith Carow, and began to earn his living as an author (writing more than thirty books in his lifetime). The couple's family grew to include six children, all of whom adored their father and his boyish

---

Times with his children were welcome retreats from what soon became a busy public life.

---

spirit. At the family home on Long Island, he romped with his brood as if he himself were still a boy of seven and was often seen racing them in wheelbarrows or leading them on hikes. It was no surprise when, years later, the White House halls held many exotic family pets and obstacle courses. Roosevelt once wrote that "a household of children . . . makes all other forms of success and achievement lose their importance."

Times with his children were welcome retreats from what soon became a busy public life.

Roosevelt worked to overcome corruption as a civil service commissioner and as a police commissioner of New York, and he served as assistant secretary of the Navy. The latter post he resigned in 1898 to lead the first U.S. volunteer cavalry regiment in the Spanish-American War. Colonel Roosevelt led his troop of "Rough Riders" to Cuba and to victory in the Battle of San Juan Heights.

Returning home as a war hero, Roosevelt's political star continued to rise. He was elected governor of New York in 1898 and became vice president of the United States just two years later. Though he had aspirations of becoming president, his time came sooner than expected. In September 1901, President William McKinley was assassinated, and Theodore Roosevelt suddenly had a monumental new responsibility.

At age forty-two, Roosevelt was the youngest president in history, but years of fighting personal and public battles had prepared him for his responsibilities. He championed the cause of conservation

The First Family: Quentin, President Roosevelt, Ted, Archie, Alice, Kermit, Edith, and Ethel. Photograph courtesy of the Library of Congress.

and battled political corruption. He set in motion the construction of the Panama Canal; built a strong, new Navy; and received the Nobel Peace Prize for his negotiations during the Russo-Japanese War. Throughout his two terms, the American public held on to him as their irrepressible leader.

After leaving the White House, Theodore Roosevelt returned to private life with equal resolve. He hunted big game in Africa and explored an uncharted river in the Amazon jungle. His voice continued to be heard in American politics; and when he died in his sleep in January of 1919, it was hard for the country to believe that the force known as Teddy Roosevelt was actually gone. He was an extraordinary man, one whom Thomas Edison called "the most striking figure in American life." This once-feeble child had challenged himself to live up to his father's name and in turn had earned the respect of not only his family, but of all America.

BORN: October 27, 1858, New York, New York

DIED: January 6, 1919, Oyster Bay, Long Island, New York

ACCOMPLISHMENTS: Vice president and president of the United States; recipient of the 1906 Nobel Peace Prize

QUOTE: "We are face to face with our destiny and we must meet it with a high and resolute courage."

Little Lights

J. Harold Gwynne

Somehow the little colored lights
    Are brighter than the rest;
Of all the lovely Christmas sights,
    The little lights are best.

The rows and strings of lights we see
    Are imaged on the snow;
But little lights upon the trees
    Shine forth with mystic glow.

They shine like jewels rich and rare,
    In red, and blue, and green;
They look like flowers, bright and fair,
    That summer days have seen.

Perhaps the little lights are blessed
    With healing, light and mild,
Because they burn and shine their best
    For Mary's little Child.

*Old-fashioned Christmas decorations make a family room
warm and inviting. Photograph by Jessie Walker.*

To a New House at Christmas

Rosemary Clifford Trott

This year and hereafter
Let every beam and rafter
Echo love and laughter.
Store up the sound of fife and drum,
Hold close new babies and the cry
Of young delight. Let children come.
Enclose much love, for people die
And years grow old. You cannot keep,
Except in mind, the footsteps gone.
The homing heart may joy or weep.
Yours is the wonder that is born
Of holding close all those who call
Your roof their own. Confide to boughs
About your eaves in spring or fall,
In June or now that life endows
A house with Christmas laughter
For now and ever after.

A blue-and-white quilt serves as a tablecloth for a cheerful holiday breakfast. Photograph by Jessie Walker.

HANDMADE HEIRLOOM

Melissa Lester with Lois Winston

THAT FAMOUS PARTRIDGE

These are the days my husband and I dreamed about. We have three children ages five and under, so this Christmas promises to be filled with joy and wonder. I am eager to make the most of this holiday season, taking time out for the little things that make lasting memories.

Decorating the Christmas tree with ornaments that are special to us is one part of our holiday preparation we especially enjoy. I have often wondered about the origin of this lovely tradition.

According to certain legends, Martin Luther actually began the tradition of decorating Christmas trees. One Christmas Eve around 1500, he placed candles on an evergreen in honor of Christ's birthday. The idea had come to him while walking through the woods and noting the beauty of the snow-dusted evergreen branches shimmering in the moonlight.

Other German families quickly adopted the custom, adding nuts, sweets, and paper roses to the trees along with the candles. Painted eggshells, cookies, and candies followed. The craft of blown glass began in Germany around the same time. Soon, a thriving cottage industry of blown-glass ornaments developed in eastern Germany. By 1700, the tradition of decorating a Christmas tree had spread from the Rhine River District throughout Germany. The custom of decorating Christmas trees probably arrived in America with early German immigrants to Pennsylvania and Ohio. When Prince Albert, Queen Victoria's German husband, introduced the custom to England, the British as well as the Americans fully adopted the custom.

In 1880, F. W. Woolworth began importing hand-cast lead and hand-blown glass Christmas ornaments from Germany to satisfy the growing American demand. And the demand was huge. Most Europeans decorated trees of four feet or less, but Americans were soon decorating trees whose branches reached from floor to ceiling.

Over time, ornaments became more elaborate and expensive. Silk and wool threads, chenille, and

The handstitched ornament features the famous partridge in his perch and took only a few hours to create.

tinsel embellishments were added. Spun-glass ornaments became popular. By 1935, America was importing more than 250 million Christmas tree ornaments a year. American companies soon recognized the market and began producing ornaments. As technology became more sophisticated, the American public conversely rediscovered an interest in handmade decorations and now many needlework and beaded ornaments, as well as youngsters' school projects, decorate family trees.

In our family, ornaments that pertain to "The

Twelve Days of Christmas" are favorites because we all love to sing the lyrics. At five, our elder son has mastered most of the words, but our two-year-old makes me smile each time he chimes in at the end with "a pear twee in a pear twee!"

Some believe the song was written as a mnemonic device to remind oppressed Christians of tenets of their faith. The partridge in a pear tree is said to represent Jesus; the two turtle doves are the two Testaments; the three French hens are faith, hope, and love; and so on. More likely, however, the song originated as a Twelfth Night game, where a leader would sing a stanza and players would repeat it, adding verses until someone made a mistake. The erring player would have to pay a penalty, perhaps offering a kiss or a sweet.

The lyrics to "The Twelve Days of Christmas" were first published in their English form in the 1780 children's book *Mirth Without Mischief*, but the song is probably much older. Clues in the song indicate that it is probably French.

A few errors have crept into our understanding of the lyrics. The four calling birds we sing about were originally the four "colly," or black, birds. And the phrase "five golden rings" actually refers to ring-necked birds like pheasants. Correcting these misconceptions restores the order of gifts to include birds for the first seven days.

This song endures as one of the most popular Christmas songs of all time, inspiring many crafts and collectibles. Handcrafted ornaments of wood, mercury glass, cloisonné, embroidery, and other forms remind us of this beloved song.

The handstitched ornament pictured above features the famous partridge in his perch and took only a few hours to create. You may easily adapt your own design to graph paper, adjusting colors and features, and then transfer it to cross-stitch fabric. When you have completed the design, you can sew the cross-stitched piece with

A beautifully stitched partridge in a pear tree is a lovely addition to a family's collection of ornaments. Design and construction courtesy of DMC. Photograph by Gerald Koser.

a backing piece, as if you were making a small pillow. This cream background works well, but a deep red would also be beautiful with gold or silver trim. When measuring for the trim, be sure to add enough extra length for the hanging loop. There are wonderful varieties of trims available; the gold braiding and tassel used in this ornament provide a touch of elegance.

This year, when each of us has finished placing our favorite ornaments on the tree, we will sing some carols and try to remember the gifts, in their proper order, in "The Twelve Days of Christmas."

Melissa Lester and Lois Winston are both freelance writers and mothers. Melissa lives in Alabama, and Lois lives in New Jersey.

Christmas is not a time or a season but a state of mind. To cherish peace and goodwill, to be plenteous in mercy, is to have the real spirit of Christmas. If we think on these things, there will be born in us a Savior and over us will shine a star sending its gleam of hope to the world.

CALVIN COOLIDGE

Beneath the Tree
Author Unknown

The crystal star was gleaming bright
From the topmost branch on Christmas night.
I sat alone, and icicles twirled
And twinkled at me from their tinsel world.
Beneath the tree, where gifts had lain,
The cross of the wooden base was plain
Through the cotton snow, and I was stirred
By a thought so true that I almost heard.
Beneath the beauty, the glitter and gloss,
No Christmas wholly conceals the Cross,
For there is a form that each must own,
Geometry of flesh and bone.
And Bethlehem's star can never die;
The heart's own cross will hold it high.

Pink roses and pearls grace this Christmas tree and fireplace mantel with pale beauty. Photograph by Jessie Walker.

A Special Invitation

TO SAVE UP TO 50% OFF THE COVER PRICE!

TERM	RETAIL VALUE	YOUR PRICE	YOU SAVE
1 year	$35.70	$19.95	$15.75
2 years	$71.40	$35.95	$35.45

My Name _____

Address _____

City _____

State _____ ZIP _____

☐ Start or Renew my own subscription   ☐ 1 year ☐ 2 years

☐ Payment enclosed   ☐ Bill me later

PREFERRED SUBSCRIBER

Yes! SEND A GIFT SUBSCRIPTION AND GIFT ANNOUNCEMENT IN MY NAME TO:

Name _____

Address _____

City _____

State _____ ZIP _____

ideals®

Your first issue will arrive in 4 to 6 weeks. Add $6 per year for Canadian and $11 per year for Foreign subscriptions, payable in U.S. funds. Limited offer. All orders subject to approval.

05-202243566

The Wonder of Christmas

Elisabeth Weaver Winstead

In manger bed
    on fragrant hay,
The precious
    Baby Jesus lay;
Gentle Mary
    proud vigil kept;
The Holy Infant
    smiling slept.

Soft lambs and sheep
    beside Him stayed,
Warm shields from chilling,
    cold winds made.
Wise Men and shepherds
    traveled afar,
Guided by rays of
    gold-gleaming star.

Heralding angels
    chorused in flight
The gladness of
    that glorious night.
Rich gifts of praise were
    given to greet
The sacred Christ Child,
    precious and sweet.

A brilliant, bright halo
    encircled above
The cradled dear Baby,
    God's gift of love.
The hopes for joy
    and peace were born,
Our wondrous gift, that
    first Christmas morn.

The doors of Saint Paul's Episcopal Church in Brookline, Massachusetts, are bright against the Christmas snow. Photograph by Dianne Dietrich/Dietrich Leis Stock Photography.

Reveries

Deborah A. Bennett

Hushed stood heaven's gentle angels,
Round the moonlight-frosted hills.
Hushed, the shepherds keeping watch
O'er flocks abiding in the fields.

Hushed, the stars in the pilgrim sky
Above celestial climes traversed.
Hushed, the Wise Men's greeting came
To mark the Savior's birth.

Hushed, with myrrh and incense sweet,
Their treasures they opened to Him.
Hushed, they heard the tidings of joy
That filled the stable dim.

All hushed as the Babe in the manger lay,
So soft in the nestling peace.
Hushed, as the streets of Bethlehem
Beneath the white wind's reveries.

*Joseph and Mary watch over the Infant Jesus, as an
angel hovers and shepherds are awed by the brilliant
star, in this painting by an unknown artist. Image
provided by Fine Art Photographic Library, Ltd.,
London/Private Collection.*

Devotions from the Heart

Pamela Kennedy

And when they were come into the house, they saw the young child with Mary his mother, and fell down, and worshipped him: and when they had opened their treasures, they presented unto him gifts; gold, and frankincense, and myrrh. — Matthew 2:11

Christmas Giving

I rushed in after a frantic day of Christmas shopping. After a brief look through the mail, I tossed it onto the end table, accidentally knocking over the Magi. (Ever since our daughter learned in first grade that the wise men didn't show up until a year or so after Christ's birth, she has forbidden us to put them anywhere near the crèche!) As I set the three kings upright again, I examined them more carefully. Each one held his gift: a little chest of gold, a vial of frankincense, a jar of myrrh. I reconsidered my recent frenzy of gift shopping. Was there something I could learn from these three little figurines?

First of all, their gifts were given with love. They had trekked a long way to find the newborn King, and, when they finally stood before Him, they fell down and worshiped.

Second, they brought gifts that cost them something, not an inexpensive trinket or bauble picked up at a strip mall along the caravan route.

Third, their gifts demonstrated an understanding of the recipient. Yes, He was just a young child, but they knew He was also a mighty king. They brought gold that spoke of royalty, frankincense that represented deity, and myrrh that may have presaged His suffering and death. These valuable gifts may have even made it possible for Joseph and Mary to finance their escape to and return from Egypt. If so, the gifts were also very practical. Was there a lesson here for me?

So often it seemed my primary goal was to check the box next to each name on my gift list, indicating that I was finished with one more recipient and could move on to the next. The joy

---

Dear Lord, may the gifts I give this Christmas be a reflection of the love You show me every day.

---

of giving, the love was maybe less than it could be.

I tried to remember times when I was really excited to give a particular person a gift. I thought of the year early in our marriage when I created handmade butcher aprons for everyone. We had little money, but I carefully chose the fabric and appliquéd different items indicative of the person's interests on the front of each apron. My husband's had a hamburger, complete with a ruffle of green lettuce peeking out from under the bun, and my father-in-law's had a black stew pot

A small table-top Christmas tree provides a focal point for the display of presents carefully wrapped. Photograph by Jessie Walker.

with red rickrack steam rising from it. They were not costly, except in time, but they communicated that I knew something about the recipient and cared about him.

Another year I put together notebooks with old photos and original poems about our parents at different stages in their lives. My own children were recently reading through the one I had given my mother, asking her how she and their grandfather had met. The gift is still being enjoyed, over thirty years later.

I recalled the special gift my own daughter had given me just a year earlier. On a very slim, college-student budget, she had secretly taken a photo of my mother and me from the back, walking arm in arm across some sand dunes. The pic-

ture, in a simple frame, brought tears to my eyes when I opened it. What a treasure!

Maybe I have let Christmas shopping become just another holiday chore when I should be looking at gifts as an expression of love and caring, to be given from the heart—a reflection of God's gift to us over two thousand years ago. Maybe I could take a lesson from the Magi and offer gifts this year that demonstrated my love, a sacrifice of time, and my understanding.

Pamela Kennedy is a freelance writer of short stories, articles, essays, and children's books. Wife of a retired naval officer and mother of three children, she has made her home on both U.S. coasts and currently resides in Honolulu, Hawaii.

One Candle

Virginia Gilman

In the darkened church on Christmas Eve,
A single candle burned,
Then flickered briefly in the night
Until the flame returned.
As the choir sang "O Holy Night"
Beside the manger scene,

The room, aglow with love and light,
Seemed peacefully serene.
Then through the silent night there rang,
From all whose hearts believed,
A prayer that every day might hold
The peace of Christmas Eve.

Christmas Grace

Miriam Snow Priebe

Dear Lord, on this, Your day of birth,
Our tree is bright with shining balls,
Our house rings out with cries of mirth,
Grandchildren play in the halls.
Throughout our home
    soft lights are gleaming;
Our table with rich food is spread;
And friends have come,
    with faces beaming,
To share with us in breaking bread.

You came, dear Lord, to humble stall;
Rough shepherds were Your guests that day.
You shared the warmth of donkey small
As You lay swaddled in the hay.

A heavenly star, bright light was bringing,
And love shone from Your mother's face;
And angel choirs on high were singing
That You had come to save our race.

Dear Lord, on this Your day of birth,
We thank You for the food we share;
We thank You for these gifts on earth;
We thank You for the clothes we wear,
For warmth, and home, and love of friends.
We thank You for the life You bring,
Eternal life that never ends.
We praise You, Savior, Christ our King!

The window of an old church building in Sister Bay, Door County, Wisconsin, frames a tall Christmas tree. Photograph by Darryl R. Beers.

Joseph's Dream

MATTHEW 1:20–24

But while he thought on these things, behold, the angel of the Lord appeared unto him in a dream, saying, Joseph, thou son of David, fear not to take unto thee Mary thy wife: for that which is conceived in her is of the Holy Ghost.

And she shall bring forth a son, and thou shalt call his name JESUS: for he shall save his people from their sins.

Now all this was done, that it might be fulfilled which was spoken of the Lord by the prophet, saying,

Behold, a virgin shall be with child, and shall bring forth a son, and they shall call his name Emmanuel, which being interpreted is, God with us.

Then Joseph being raised from sleep did as the angel of the Lord had bidden him, and took unto him his wife.

Joseph receives the news imparted to him by an angel in a dream, in a painting by Giotto di Bondone, entitled THE DREAM OF JOACHIM, in the Scrovegni Chapel, Padua, Italy. Image provided by Cameraphoto/Art Resource, New York.

The Nativity

LUKE 2:1–7

And it came to pass in those days, that there went out a decree from Caesar Augustus, that all the world should be taxed. (And this taxing was first made when Cyrenius was governor of Syria.) And all went to be taxed, every one into his own city.

And Joseph also went up from Galilee, out of the city of Nazareth, into Judaea, unto the city of David, which is called Bethlehem; (because he was of the house and lineage of David:) To be taxed with Mary his espoused wife, being great with child.

And so it was, that, while they were there, the days were accomplished that she should be delivered. And she brought forth her firstborn son, and wrapped him in swaddling clothes, and laid him in a manger; because there was no room for them in the inn.

Angels praise the newborn Savior and share the news of His birth with shepherds, in this painting entitled THE NATIVITY, by Giotto di Bondone, in the Scrovegni Chapel, Padua, Italy. Image provided by Cameraphoto/Art Resource, New York.

The Adoration of the Magi

MATTHEW 2:1–2, 7–11

*N*ow when Jesus was born in Bethlehem of Judaea in the days of Herod the king, behold, there came wise men from the east to Jerusalem, Saying, Where is he that is born King of the Jews? for we have seen his star in the east, and are come to worship him.

Then Herod, when he had privily called the wise men, inquired of them diligently what time the star appeared. And he sent them to Bethlehem, and said, Go and search diligently for the young child; and when ye have found him, bring me word again, that I may come and worship him also.

When they had heard the king, they departed; and, lo, the star, which they saw in the east, went before them, till it came and stood over where the young child was.

When they saw the star, they rejoiced with exceeding great joy. And when they were come into the house, they saw the young child with Mary his mother, and fell down, and worshipped him: and when they had opened their treasures, they presented unto him gifts; gold, and frankincense, and myrrh.

The three kings acknowledge the young infant as Savior in the painting by Giotto di Bondone, entitled ADORATION OF THE MAGI, in the Scrovegni Chapel, Padua, Italy. Image provided by Alinari/Art Resource, New York.

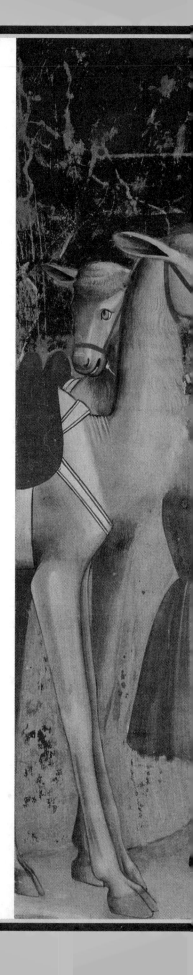

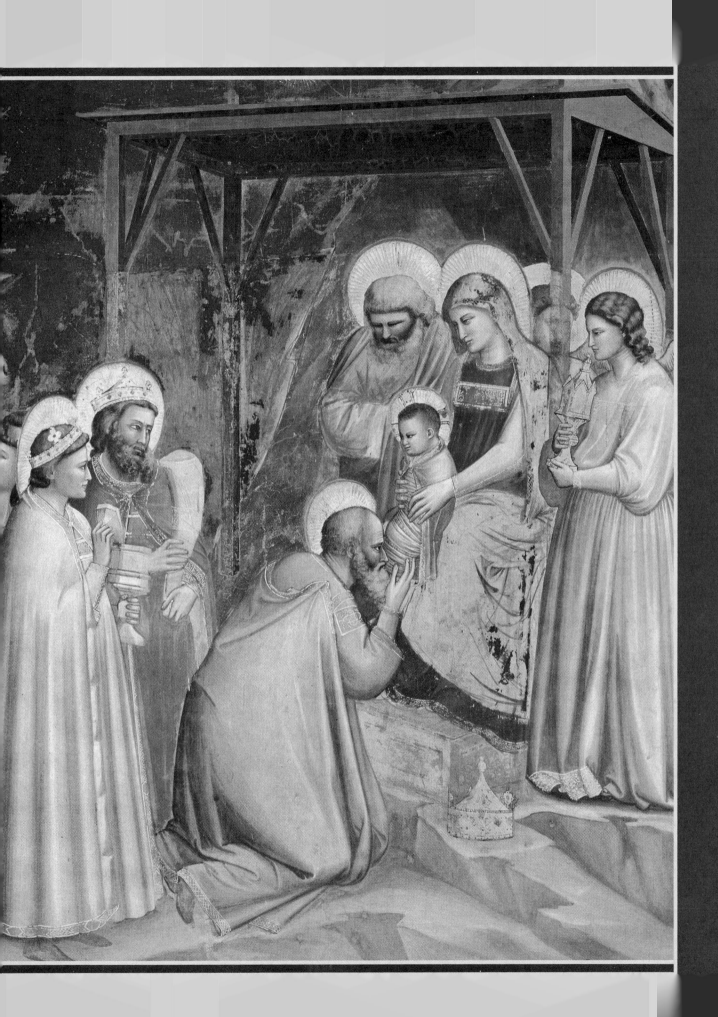

Presentation at the Temple

LUKE 2: 25–32

And, behold, there was a man in Jerusalem, whose name was Simeon; and the same man was just and devout, waiting for the consolation of Israel: and the Holy Ghost was upon him. And it was revealed unto him by the Holy Ghost, that he should not see death, before he had seen the Lord's Christ.

And he came by the Spirit into the temple: and when the parents brought in the child Jesus, to do for him after the custom of the law, Then took he him up in his arms, and blessed God, and said, Lord, now lettest thou thy servant depart in peace, according to thy word: For mine eyes have seen thy salvation, Which thou hast prepared before the face of all people; A light to lighten the Gentiles, and the glory of thy people Israel.

Simeon recognizes the fulfillment of God's plan for salvation through Jesus in this painting, entitled THE PRESENTATION OF CHRIST IN THE TEMPLE, by Giotto di Bondone, in the Scrovegni Chapel, Padua, Italy. Image provided by Cameraphoto/Art Resource, New York.

Flight into Egypt

MATTHEW 2:13–15, 19–21

And when they were departed, behold, the angel of the Lord appeareth to Joseph in a dream, saying, Arise, and take the young child and his mother, and flee into Egypt, and be thou there until I bring thee word: for Herod will seek the young child to destroy him.

When he arose, he took the young child and his mother by night, and departed into Egypt: And was there until the death of Herod: that it might be fulfilled which was spoken of the Lord by the prophet, saying, Out of Egypt have I called my son.

But when Herod was dead, behold, an angel of the Lord appeareth in a dream to Joseph in Egypt, Saying, Arise, and take the young child and his mother, and go into the land of Israel: for they are dead which sought the young child's life. And he arose, and took the young child and his mother, and came into the land of Israel.

Joseph leads his new family into Egypt to avoid the wrath of Herod, in this painting entitled FLIGHT INTO EGYPT, by Giotto di Bondone. Image provided by Scala/Art Resource, New York.

IDEALS DEBUT ISSUE

CHRISTMAS 1944

These two poems are reprinted from the first issue of IDEALS magazine. Their message still speaks to the present generation of IDEALS readers. We invite you to continue to share in the celebration of sixty years of dedication to family, country, and God. Best wishes for a happy holiday season from everyone at IDEALS.

Let Us Keep Christmas

Grace Noll Crowell

Whatever else be lost among the years,
Let us keep Christmas still a shining thing:
Whatever doubts assail us, or what fears,
Let us hold close one day, remembering
Its poignant meaning for the hearts of men.
Let us get back our childlike faith again.

Wealth may have taken wings,
Yet still there are clear windowpanes
To glow with candlelight;
There are boughs for garlands and a tinsel star

To tip some little fir tree's lifted height.
There is no heart too heavy or too sad,
But some small gift of love can make it glad.

And there are home-sweet rooms
Where laughter rings,
And we can sing the carols as of old.
Above the eastern hills a white star swings;
There is an ancient story to be told;
There are kind words and cheering words to say:
Let us be happy on the Christ Child's day.

The Star

Thomas P. Carrol

Men were dust and the world was dark
When a star appeared in the sky,
Transforming this dust into children of God,
A miracle working on high.

It lighted the fires of faith and love,
Instilled hope in the hearts of men,
Marking the dawn of a new way of life—
"The Star of Bethlehem!"

Down through the ages has come the glow
Of this radiant Christmas star;
In the lighted heavens of man's ideals,
Its brilliancy carried far.

It represents the highest goal
That all nations should attain;
O discouraged, wearied, and war-torn world,
Reach out for this star again.

Stained-glass windows illuminate the night at a church in Lunenburg, Vermont. Photograph by W. Pote/H. Armstrong Roberts.

Christmas Reflection

Sarah C. Merrell

I hope my heart has heard the song
The shepherd heard that night.
I hope my heart has found the star
The Wise Men kept in sight.
Then maybe it will find its way
To the quiet manger too,
So the heart can kneel in worship,
Bringing gifts sincere and true.
My heart can bring no wealth of gold,
Nor perfumes rich and sweet;
But let it bring humility
And lay it at His feet.
It may bring loyalty and truth,
With love wrapped all around;
Then, having looked upon the Child,
Rejoice with gladsome sound.
For shepherds went upon their way,
Rejoicing loud and clear.
They spread good tidings so
That my heart, too, might hear.

A Christmas Prayer

Mabel Clare Thomas

I do not ask for riches, Lord,
In this my Christmas prayer,
Nor do I seek fame's transient glow,
However bright and fair.
The gift I seek is richer far,
Purer, undefiled—
Oh, give me, Lord, the love and trust
In the heart of a little child.

*The snow-covered forest glows with the colors of
sunset in this painting, entitled* Sunset through the Forest,
*by Laszlo Neogrady (1861–1942). Image provided by
Fine Art Photographic Library, Ltd., London/Burlington Paintings.*

Thou Whose Birth

A. C. Swinburne

Thou whose birth on earth
Angels sang to men
While the stars made mirth,
Savior, at Thy birth
This day born again;

As this night was bright
With Thy cradle-ray,
Very light of light,
Turn the wild world's night
To Thy perfect day.

Bid our peace increase,
Thou that madest morn;
Bid oppressions cease;
Bid the night be peace;
Bid the day be born.

Always Christmas

Kay Hoffman

There'll always be a Christmas
        Wherever our path may lead
As long as hearts reach out
        To help someone in need.

As long as little children kneel
        Beside their bed to pray,
"God bless the Baby Jesus,
        And help me be good each day."

There'll always be a Christmas
        With hope and peace again,
As long as there is caring
        And goodwill toward all men.

As long as there is faith and love
        To keep hearts warm and kind,
No matter where our path may lead,
        There'll be a Christmastime.

*Inset: A cardinal finds a safe perch in winter snow.
Photograph by Gay Bumgarner.*

*The sun glimmers through snow-covered balsams in Peninsula State Park,
Door County, Wisconsin. Photograph by Darryl R. Beers.*

Christmas Bells

Mamie Ozburn Odum

The bells peal forth
    on Christmas Day,
Pleading the world
    to kneel and pray.
Each stroke comes sweet
The world to greet
With peace, sweet peace,
    on Christmas Day.

Christmas has come
    throughout the land
And brings the Christ-child
    to every man.
The story old, yet new,
A story old, but true,
Of peace, sweet peace,
    on Christmas Day.

The chimes peal out
    along the way
To bless the land
    both night and day,
A chant so sweet,
All hearts to greet
With peace, sweet peace,
    on Christmas Day.

Silently I pray, I know the need,
"Give us peace on earth," I plead.
"Remove the wrong,
Fill hearts with song
And peace, sweet peace,
    on Christmas Day."

The bells ring out with great elation
And reach the heart of every nation,
The right will grow,
Wrong fail, we know,
With peace, sweet peace,
    on Christmas Day.

The lights of a Victorian house welcome visitors.
Photograph by William H. Johnson.

The Merry Bells of Christmastime

Anton J. Stoffle

The merry bells of Christmastime
Ring joyously to send the word;
In solemn notes of earthly cheer,
About the world their truth is heard.

Within their rhythm and their time,
Somehow they strike a harmony,
Though separated by the miles,
Bound only by humanity.

Yet in those ancient bells that chime,
A certain message seems to cling,
Uniting every Christian heart
To Jesus, Savior, Lord, and King.

Oh, let them ring, those Christmas bells;
Let every mortal heart rejoice,
For God, the Father, wills it so
That we might hear His gentle voice.

Carolers

Louise Preston Greene

It's a radiant world this Christmas night,
As the darkness glows with brilliant light
From homes where faith and Christmas cheer
Are the blessed part of this time of year.
Then, suddenly on the frost-crisp air,
Bright carolers' songs ring out everywhere
With "Hark! The herald angels sing
With glory to the newborn King."
And in our hearts we join with them
The star-led trek to Bethlehem.

A brightly decorated Christmas tree is the background for a festive display of carolers. Photograph by William H. Johnson.

TRAVELER'S DIARY

D. Fran Morley

JOHN F. KENNEDY CENTER FOR THE PERFORMING ARTS
WASHINGTON, D.C.

In a city filled with monuments to famous Americans, the Kennedy Center for the Performing Arts is unique in that it is an ever-changing, living memorial. While preparing for my trip to our nation's capital, I learned that the desire for a national cultural center dates as far back as our first president, George Washington. But it was not until 1958 that President Dwight D. Eisenhower signed legislation creating a National Cultural Center. President John F. Kennedy then took the lead in raising funds for its construction after becoming president. Shortly after Kennedy's assassination in 1963, Congress designated the Center as a memorial and named it in his honor. So, even though the Kennedy Center honors one president, it fulfills the dreams of at least two others.

For years, my dream had been to see a performance of the National Symphony Orchestra at the Kennedy Center, but I was pleased to discover that the Center is open daily for tours that allow visitors to see the beautiful theaters and galleries and even enjoy a free midday concert. Since its opening in 1971, the Center has presented the best the world has to offer in all forms of the performing arts and is one of the most visited buildings in Washington.

When I arrived, I discovered that guides conduct tours in eleven different languages, making the Center accessible to an international audience. Obviously, Washington is an international city, but having multilingual guides is also very appropriate because individuals and countries from around the world have donated art and other items to the Center in Kennedy's memory.

From the front plaza, my tour group entered through the Hall of States and walked along the wide red carpet beneath flags from all fifty states, five U.S. territories, and the District of Columbia. Starting with Delaware's, the flags are hung in the order in which each state entered the Union.

The largest theater on the main level is the famed Concert Hall.

The Hall of States opens onto the spectacular Grand Foyer, which the guide said is one of the largest rooms in the world, at sixty feet high and 630 feet long. The Grand Foyer is the lobby for the Center's three main theaters, but it is much more than just that. The room sparkles with light streaming in through tall windows overlooking the Potomac and from the glow of eighteen massive crystal chandeliers, Sweden's gift to the Center. Tremendous mirrors—nine feet wide and fifty-eight feet tall—line a wall, accented by twenty huge brass planters. Like so much of the Center's art and decor, these items were also gifts: the mirrors came from Belgium and the planters from India.

In the middle of the Grand Foyer, we paused before an impressive bronze bust of President Kennedy and took a few minutes to look over an interactive audio-visual exhibit of highlights from his life and quotes from his most memorable speeches.

Before entering the theaters, we walked the entire length of the Grand Foyer and into the Hall of Nations, which parallels the Hall of States.

A sixty-foot scaffold is required to rearrange the flags.

Here, hanging in alphabetical order, are flags from every country with which the U.S. has diplomatic relations. It was interesting to learn that if a country has a name change, a sixty-foot scaffold is required to rearrange the flags. When the states of the former Soviet Union became independent, work crews had to find a way to add twelve new flags to the display.

Our guide ushered us through the three theaters on the Center's main level. The smallest, the Eisenhower Theater, features a red-and-black handwoven stage curtain presented by the people of Canada. A gorgeous red-and-gold silk curtain from Japan and a snowflake-shaped crystal chandelier from Austria highlight the elegant red Opera House Theater. This lovely theater is the setting for the annual Kennedy Center Honors that recognizes lifetime achievements in the arts.

The largest theater on the main level is the famed Concert Hall, to which I would return for that evening's symphony performance. Nearly seven hundred high school, college, and community organizations in the United States, Canada, England, and Japan donated funds to build this stage, which has since been graced with thousands of school performances. In the empty theater, I marveled at the resplendent crystal chandeliers

The beautiful foyer of the Kennedy Center is lit by eighteen Orrefors crystal chandeliers and matching sconces, gifts from Sweden. Photograph courtesy of John F. Kennedy Center for the Performing Arts.

and imagined myself seated here as the lights dim and the curtain rises.

After the tour, I strolled along the wide top-level terraces that flank the Center and enjoyed one of the best views in the city. I thought about one of Kennedy's quotes that is displayed in the Grand Foyer: "I'm sure that after the dust of centuries has passed over our cities, we too will be remembered, not for our victories or defeats in battles or in politics, but for our contribution to the human spirit."

I know that my spirit, and I am sure that of others, was uplifted by my visit to the Kennedy Center for the Performing Arts.

When not gallivanting around the country, travel writer Fran Morley spends time with her husband, Tom, and their cat, Gracie, in beautiful Fairhope, Alabama.

Christmas Chimes

Kate Strauss Shibley

Ring bells! Joy impart!
Every eager, hungry heart
Yearns to catch that angel song;
Ages echo it along.
It halts the throng
With listening ear,
Inspiration new each year.
Sing it. Live it, once again:
"Peace on earth, goodwill to men."

The Message of Christmas Bells

Mabel Clare Thomas

Once more the bells of Christmas
Are ringing sweet and clear;
Once more our hearts are lifted up
And filled with hope and cheer,
For friendship knows no barriers
Of distance, time, or space,
And loving thoughts can wing their way
To any clime or place.

Each year the message of the bells,
Over mountain, plain, or sea,
Reminds us love is born anew,
Steadfast, tender, strong, and true,
Wherever we may be.

A piano and a tree decorated with antique ornaments await a family's celebration of the Christmas season. Photograph by Larry LeFever/Grant Heilman.

Collector's Corner

Maud Dawson

Glass Christmas Bells

When I was a child, visiting my best friend's house was always fun, but being invited indoors was a special occasion. I enjoyed the careful walk through the living room because on a dainty, curved-leg table sat something I had never before seen— a tiny bell of soft, creamy glass decorated with a scene of a couple riding in a red sleigh. It was the most beautiful object in the entire room.

After a few trips indoors, I found the courage to ask my friend's mother about that special bell and was told—after the admonition to never, never pick it up—that the glass was called "custard satin glass" and the title of the scene was, appropriately, "Going Home."

Each year during the Christmas holidays, I made certain to visit my my friend's mother and ask her what new bell she had added to her Christmas display. I liked to hear her discussions of the types of glass—names like "satin opal," "milk glass," "amethyst carnival," "Rosalene," and "French opalescent."

One year she had a custard-glass bell that depicted a snow-covered church and was titled "Christmas Morn." There was a bright red poin-

*The title of this bell's design is as lovely as the bell itself—*Magnolia Blush on French Opalescent. *Photograph courtesy of Fenton Art Glass Company, Williamstown, West Virginia.*

settia on an opal satin bell another year. But my favorite was one from the Christmas Fantasy series, in opal satin glass, that showed a young girl asleep in an armchair in her pajamas.

Prompted by my childhood delight with my best friend's mother's holiday display of bells, I did some research and learned about the beauty and varieties of glass bells.

Glass bells were produced and readily available in the United States in the 1800s. The first ones were table bells for the wealthy, who summoned servants during meals. Then souvenir bells and commemorative bells of specific events became popular. As increasingly sophisticated methods shortened production, pressed glass became popular. Today, collectors can choose from many types of antique bells as well as an array of lovely ones made by contemporary artisans, whether they limit their pursuit to holiday selections or include other categories.

When I begin setting up holiday decorations for my own family today, my favorite small piece, with its special place on the mantel, is a "Birds of Winter" bell showing bluebirds in front of a snowy landscape, on "opal satin." I look forward to adding more each year.

RINGING IN THE HOLIDAYS

If you enjoy the sparkle of a glass bell, the following information may be helpful in beginning your collection.

CUT-GLASS BELLS

•*Brilliant Period, 1876–1915:* Prior to the 1880s, very few cut-glass bells were produced. Beginning with the year of America's Centennial, beautiful cut-glass bells were added to elaborate table settings of cut glass in the homes of the wealthy. These were initially used to summon servants; but, with the advent of the use of electricity, these bells became primarily decorative. The designs of these bells had detailed geometric patterns. Their handles were usually glass or silver.

•*Flower Period, 1906–1920s:* Cut and engraved flowers began to appear on bells, along with other objects from nature.

PRESSED-GLASS BELLS

Less costly than cut glass, pressed glass bells became available during the Flower Period. Free-blown, mold-blown, and mold-pressed glass offered increased variations on the types of designs available.

ENGRAVED AND ETCHED-GLASS BELLS

Blown glass bells of thin glass blanks were often engraved during the late nineteenth and early twentieth century. Fine examples of etched glass continue to be popular with collectors.

FAMILIAR AMERICAN COMPANIES

The values of the early bells from these companies start in the hundreds and reach into the thousands of dollars.

•*C. Dorflinger & Sons, 1865–1964:* This company's cut-glass bells had three distinctive designs on the tops of the handles—strawberry diamonds, radial miters, and raised buttons.

•*Fenton Art Glass, 1905–Present:* The oldest American glass company in continuous operation produced its first bell in carnival glass for the Elks

These exquisite glass bells are beautiful contemporary versions of delicate table bells. Photograph courtesy of Fenton Art Glass Company, Williamstown, West Virginia.

convention in Atlantic City in 1911. It now produces more blown- and pressed-glass bells than any other American company. Some of its popular collections include a yearly holiday series.

•*Fostoria Glass, 1891–1986:* In addition to producing bells that match its stemware, this company began producing a series of holiday bells in 1977. One of their loveliest patterns is a frosted bell with engraved Christmas scenes.

•*T. G. Hawkes, 1880–1962:* This company made exquisite cut-glass crystal and often salvaged broken stemware by turning it into bells.

•*Libbey Glass, 1892–Present:* During the World's Columbian Exposition of 1893 in Chicago, this company produced many souvenir bells, a subcategory of bell collection still popular today.

•*Pilgrim Glass, 1949–2001:* This company is known for blown bells in many colors with clear handles.

•*Seneca Glass, 1891–1983:* In the 1960s and 70s, this company made bells with thin blown lead glass, which featured hollow handles.

Who can be insensible to the outpourings of good feeling and the honest interchange of affectionate attachment which abound at this season of the year? A Christmas family-party! We know nothing in nature more delightful! There seems a magic in the very name of Christmas.

—CHARLES DICKENS

An Old-Fashioned Christmas

Elisabeth Weaver Winstead

Let's have an old-fashioned Christmas;
What a day of delight it will be,
Hanging wreaths of spruce and cedar,
Bringing home the fresh, green tree.

Candlelight shines by each window,
Sprigs of holly on mantel and door,
Sweet aroma of gingerbread cookies,
Pies and puddings baked by the score.

Bright sleds skim frozen hilltops,
Velvet snowflakes in radiance beam,
Ice skaters glide like quicksilver
In the moonlight's golden gleam.

Make it an old-fashioned Christmas!
May each waiting heart feel the glow
That grows with the ringing of sleigh bells,
Drifting over the soft-silvered snow.

A beautiful vintage album holds many Christmas memories.
Photograph by Jessie Walker.

December's Visitor

Eileen Spinelli

Christmas
comes calling
with pageants and wings,
with ribbons and holly
and popcorn on strings,
with boxes of tinsel,
with chestnuts and pies.
Christmas comes calling
with joy in her eyes.

Christmas
comes calling
with carols and bells,
with sparkling trees
and gingerbread smells,
with snowflakes and starlight
through cities and farms.
Chrismas comes calling
with peace in her arms.

These three children are delighted with the decorations on their tree, in this painting entitled DECORATING THE TREE, by an unknown artist. Image provided by Fine Art Photographic Library, Ltd., London/Private Collection.

REMEMBER WHEN

Joan Donaldson

GLADLY THEY SANG

My family's holiday celebration always began and ended with the Robert Shaw Chorale. My father slipped the finely grooved record from its dust jacket, wiped it with a flannel cloth, and placed it on the turntable's spindle. The needle head lifted and dropped onto the record. The first seconds of static ceased when the voices of the chorale opened with a familiar medley of carols.

From that moment, throughout the holiday weeks, the pink and white dust jacket remained propped up against my family's record player and decorated that corner of the living room. On the jacket, a cluster of children dressed in variously colored woolen coats and caps held sheet music and sang, while snow sparkled behind them.

Under somber skies I trudged home from school, pink cheeked from the raw winds. But the afternoon brightened when I pushed open the storm door and heard those recorded voices gladly singing while my mother hummed along. Steam from cooling cookies fogged the kitchen windows. Trays of Scottish shortbread, toffee squares, and Russian teacakes waited to be packed into tins. My mother baked the fussier cookies while my brother and I were at school, but we created the cut out cookies on a Saturday close to Christmas.

My family had learned the progression of the recorded carols, and my brother and I could sing "O come all ye faithful, joyful and triumphant, O come ye, O come ye to Bethlehem!" while cutting out stars, snowmen, and Christmas bells sprigged with holly. I stood tiptoe on a stool, braids dangling down my back while my brother and I took turns rolling, stamping, and sifting colored sugar over the cookies. Sampling the sugar left red and green streaks on our tongues that could only be hidden

---

The joyous carols sung by the chorale flowed through that night.

---

by tasting scraps of cookie dough. Our voices continued with Martin Luther's cradle song and "God Rest Ye Merry, Gentlemen" before the medley of carols ended.

Each evening the record rested, while I repeated the carols on my piano. My teacher chose simple arrangements that my eight-year-old fingers could master. I imagined that I was a splendid pianist accompanying a heavenly choir that sounded like the Robert Shaw chorale.

As the school days edged closer to the Christmas program, my classmates and I rehearsed the words to "The Friendly Beasts." No one was brave enough to sing a solo, but clusters of us were chosen to represent each of the animals that welcomed Baby Jesus. The morning of Christmas Eve, we arrived at school with slicked-back hair and shiny shoes that heightened our holiday spirit. My third-grade class marched into the spacious audito-

This young family shares a special time beside their Christmas tree. Photograph from Retrofile/H. Armstrong Roberts.

rium where parents waited expectantly. Along with the other children, we squirmed on the wooden seats lined up in front.

When my class filed onto the stage, we arranged ourselves in rows under a wide arch, and the image of the children on the pink and white dust jacket flickered in my mind. My classmates lacked the luster of those carolers and no snow fell behind us as we sang. But the excitement of Christmas filled our voices and hearts as we raced through the words.

After a reception with punch and cookies, my classmates and I skipped home, eager for a vacation. My brother and I endured the afternoon of waiting as we entertained ourselves with one early Christmas present. The click and the drop of the record needles repeated itself as my mother drowned out our play with the music of the chorale.

Clothed in a velvet dress with a lace collar and fresh ribbons in my braids, I sat, eyes shining, as we finally drove through the dimly lit residential streets to my grandparents' house where my extended family would congregate. Snowflakes splattered against the windshield. In my dark green wool coat and cap, I now looked like one of the carolers on the dust jacket. I heard the voices from the record in my head. Like a part in a fugue, the joyous carols sung by the chorale flowed through that night and the remainder of the holidays. Their notes blended and swelled with the excitement of Christmas, the glad gathering of family, and the celebration that lasted until New Year's Day.

After taking down our Christmas tree, my mother slid the record into its pink and white jacket and tucked it back into the stack of albums beneath the record player. In later years, other Christmas records joined that section of albums, but none ever gained the honor given to the Robert Shaw Chorale. Those joyous arrangements and harmonies still echo in my mind.

FAMILY RECIPES

SNOWBALLS
Lydia Miller, Garnett, Kansas

3 tablespoons butter, softened
1/2 cup creamy peanut butter
1 cup confectioners' sugar
1 pound white bark coating

In a large bowl, stir butter into peanut butter. Add confectioners' sugar, mixing well. Shape into one-inch balls and place on a cookie sheet lined with waxed paper. Chill for 30 minutes.

Melt white bark coating according to directions on package. With a toothpick, dip chilled balls into white coating and place on waxed paper. Allow to harden. Makes 18 snowballs.

ITALIAN CREAM CAKE
Frances T. Hite, Fargo, North Dakota

2 cups all-purpose flour
1 teaspoon baking soda
1/2 cup vegetable oil
3/4 cup butter, softened, divided
2 cups granulated sugar
5 eggs, separated
1 cup buttermilk
2 teaspoons vanilla
1 cup shredded coconut
1 cup chopped walnuts
1 8-ounce package cream cheese, softened
4 cups confectioners' sugar

Preheat oven to 350°F. In a medium bowl, sift flour with baking soda; set aside. In a large mixing bowl, cream oil and 1/2 cup butter with sugar until light. Add egg yolks and beat well. Alternately add flour mixture and buttermilk to butter mixture, beating after each addition, just until combined. Add 1 teaspoon vanilla. Stir in coconut and walnuts. In a separate bowl, beat egg whites until stiff peaks form; fold into coconut mixture. Pour batter into 3 greased and lightly floured 9-inch pans and bake for 25 minutes, or until wooden toothpick inserted in center comes out clean. Cool on racks 10 minutes; turn out and cool completely.

To make frosting, in a large bowl, combine cream cheese and remaining 1/4 cup butter with confectioners' sugar. Stir in remaining 1 teaspoon vanilla. Beat until smooth. Spread frosting between layers, on sides, and on top. Makes a 9-inch, 3-layer cake.

Coconut Cream Cake

Lou O. Knight, Forest, Mississippi

- 3 cups all-purpose flour
- 2 teaspoons baking powder
- 1 cup butter, softened
- 2½ cups plus 1 tablespoon granulated sugar, divided
- 3 eggs
- 1 cup milk
- 2 teaspoons vanilla, divided
- 2 teaspoons lemon extract, divided
- ½ teaspoon plus 2 drops butter flavoring
- ½ cup water
- 2 cups whipping cream
- 6 cups shredded coconut

Preheat oven 350°F. In a medium bowl, sift flour and baking powder; set aside. In a large bowl, cream butter with sugar until light. Add eggs 1 at a time, beating after each addition. Alternately add flour mixture and milk to butter mixture, stirring after each addition. Stir in 1 teaspoon vanilla, 1 teaspoon lemon extract, and ½ teaspoon butter flavoring. Spread batter evenly into 3 greased and lightly floured 9-inch round cake pans and bake 30 minutes or until wooden toothpick inserted in center comes out clean. Cool on racks 10 minutes; turn out and cool completely. In a small saucepan, combine water and 1 tablespoon sugar; bring to a boil. Reduce heat and simmer 3 minutes. Drizzle sugar mixture over each cake layer.

To make frosting, in a large bowl, beat whipping cream until soft peaks form, gradually adding ½ cup sugar. Stir in 1 teaspoon vanilla, 1 teaspoon lemon extract, and 2 drops butter flavoring. Stir in 3 cups coconut. Spread frosting between layers and sprinkle each with about ½ cup coconut. Spread remaining frosting and sprinkle remaining coconut on top and sides. Makes a 9-inch, 3-layer cake.

Coconut Pie

Mary Dove, Gainesville, Georgia

- 2 cups granulated sugar
- 4 tablespoons all-purpose flour
- 4 eggs, beaten
- ½ cup butter, melted
- 1 7-ounce package shredded coconut
- 2 unbaked, 8-inch pie shells

Preheat oven to 350°F. In a large mixing bowl, combine flour and sugar; stir in eggs and butter. Fold coconut into sugar mixture. Pour mixture evenly into pie shells. Bake 35 minutes or until browned and firm. Makes 2 pies.

These winter-white holiday foods will add more delicious moments to your holiday festivities. We would love to try your favorite recipe too. Send a typed copy to Ideals Publications, 535 Metroplex Drive, Suite 250, Nashville, Tennessee 37211. Payment will be provided for each recipe published.

FROM MY GARDEN JOURNAL

Lisa Ragan

PEAR TREES

My family and friends receive gifts from my garden at Christmastime, and their warm responses have inspired me to keep the tradition going year after year. This year I set aside my pear harvest for presents—baskets of dried pears, canned pears with ginger and spice, and even fresh pears for the neighbors. An excellent source of fruit to be given away or kept for one's own enjoyment, pear trees have long been favored by gardeners.

FRUIT OF THE GODS

The European pear, also called the common pear, originated in southeastern Europe and the Caucasian mountains but soon found its way to ancient Greece, where Homer dubbed the pear the "fruit of the gods." The original common pear produced edible fruit that was small, dry, and gritty. But monks in Italy during the Renaissance were among those who developed new varieties that produced better fruit. The pear came to the New World with the colonists, who used the fruit for food, the wood for furniture, and the leaves for yellow dye. Thomas Jefferson grew seventeen varieties of the European pear in his Monticello fruit orchards.

The vast number of pear varieties available today include ornamental trees, which do not produce edible fruit, as well as Asian pears, which have their own characteristics and myriad varieties. Of the European pear varieties, those particularly well-suited for the backyard gardener are Moonglow, Bartlett, Seckel, D'Anjou, and Bosc.

THE COMMON PEAR

The common pear, *Pyrus communis*, produces a deciduous tree with branches that grow sharply upward. The tree's glossy, dark green leaves have a leathery texture, and its fruit has a fleshy body that surrounds a core of seeds. Skin color can vary from yellow,

THE PEAR TREE

gold, green, and bronze to deep russet and red. Standard trees typically reach heights of fifteen to twenty feet and take from eight to ten years to produce fruit, although dwarf varieties produce smaller specimens that bear fruit in three to five years. The standard common pear tree has a life expectancy between sixty and one hundred years.

PEARS WITH PICKY POLLEN

Because pear trees do not self-pollinate and bees prefer other blossoms, pear trees must be planted in groups of two or more twenty feet apart. A different but compatible variety must be selected as the pollinizer. The Magness variety, for example, has sterile pollen and cannot pollinate other trees, while Bartlett and Seckel will not cross-pollinate each other.

GROWING PRETTY PEARS

Plant seedlings in a sunny location that has well-drained, slightly acidic soil. Pear seedlings can be planted in autumn in warm climate zones and in spring in cooler regions. The soil should be worked around the roots to eliminate air pockets. Pear trees need adequate moisture and winters lacking extreme cold. Training the tree on a trellis, fence, or wall, can help to control the upward tilt of the branches.

THE REWARDS OF PATIENCE

Standard pear trees bear fruit after eight to ten years, while dwarf varieties bear fruit sooner. One to three weeks after the mature tree blossoms in the spring, June Drop may occur, wherein the tree spontaneously drops excess young fruit, usually of lesser quality. If June Drop does not occur, fruit should be thinned before midsummer to one pear per cluster. Depending on the variety, pears can be harvested anytime from July through October. Unlike most fruits, which ripen best on the tree, pears should be picked before they are fully ripe. Proper ripening will ensure optimum flavor, and the time and process will vary depending on the variety.

PESTS AND DISEASE

Pear trees can be tempting to the codling moth (in caterpillar form), snout beetle, and psylla. Some of the most common diseases that can affect pear trees are fire blight, pear scab, and canker. The best defense against pests and diseases is prevention, which can include selecting blight-resistant varieties, fertilizing sparingly, and pruning lightly once a year.

I began growing pears not long after I tasted the difference between the waxy specimens at the grocery store and a home-grown pear perfectly mellowed. The delicious taste, texture, and aroma of the latter inspired me to plant my own backyard mini-orchard, which now provides a harvest of healthy fruit. And although most of my pears are this year destined to become Christmas presents, I left some fruit on the trees to provide a midwinter treat for visiting songbirds. Perhaps I'll even attract a partridge to my pear tree!

Lisa Ragan, with the help of her son, Trenton, tends her small but mighty garden in Nashville, Tennessee.

Christmas Message

Luella Bender Carr

Beside the doorway a wreath is hung
Of cedar and cones with a tinsel bow,
And a cluster of miniature bells is swung
To tinkle a welcome. Now the snow,
Silently falling, tips with white
Each spray of cedar or tasseled pine;
And covers the doorstep snug and tight
With a snowy coverlet, smooth and fine.
Through the window, lamplight gleams
Warm and golden; its fingers seek
To reach beyond the pane. It seems
The night is articulate, waiting to speak.
Quietly I stand until,
All around in the hush, I hear
That age-old message of "Peace, goodwill"
Breathed into my listening ear.

*Pine trees wear their cloaks of winter snow at
Summer Lake Inn, Oregon. Photograph by Dennis Frates.*

THROUGH MY WINDOW

Pamela Kennedy

RUINING CHRISTMAS?

Whenever we try to add something new to our Christmas celebration or delete something old from it, we run into the objections of our daughter who complains, "But that will ruin Christmas!" She has the notion that only by keeping things exactly the same, year after year, can we annually recapture the joy and excitement of this, her favorite holiday. While I appreciate the way she cherishes family rituals, I think she has a bit to learn about the real value of traditions. Last year our Christmas tree became an excellent lesson.

A child of the Pacific Northwest, I never doubted that a freshly cut Douglas fir was the key to Christmas cheer. I remember the intoxicating scent of evergreen filling the corners of our home on the day my father set up the tree. Each morning, I would bury my face in the pungent boughs and breathe in the very essence of the Christmas season. In the evenings I would lie on my back with my head under the tree and gaze up through its branches, pretending I was in a forest filled with holiday grandeur. I was, in short, a true believer in the importance of a live tree.

Even after I married and the Navy conspired to have us spend Christmases in places like San Diego and Honolulu, where bushy Douglas firs were costly and difficult to find, my husband knew better than to suggest we get something else. That is, until the year we moved to Wisconsin. With three young children in a two-story wood frame house, we realized a dry Christmas tree could be a dangerous fire hazard. Very reluctantly, I agreed to purchase an artificial tree. But it had to look real, I determined, and we would get a wreath made of fir and pine boughs for the evergreen

78

scent. My husband and I searched until we found an artificial tree that met our standards; then, with a bit of sadness and resignation, I decorated it. To my surprise Christmas was an especially joyous time that year, filled with happy children, beautiful music, and a tree looking, if not smelling, like it had just been plucked from its forest home. A new tradition had begun and, although I can't remember why any longer, we named our little tree Bartholomew.

For twenty years, Bartholomew Tree stood as faithful guardian over our holiday festivities. Last year it became evident that his needles were sparse, his wire branches bent, and he had taken on a definite droop. It was time to replace the tree.

Happily, we discovered that since our purchase of Bartholomew, the artificial tree industry

The day our daughter arrived for Christmas break, we held our breath.

had made great advances. We found a gorgeous, realistic-looking tree that was not only taller than our old one, but wider and thicker as well. And, as an added bonus, it had all the lights already placed on the branches! Once we had our new tree in place and decorated, we were delighted with the results. But we were sure our daughter, who was away at college, would fear the imminent ruin of Christmas. And that is when my husband came up with a delightful plan. He disposed of old Bartholomew, except for the eighteen-inch uppermost section. This he mounted on a block of wood. We decorated it with miniature birds and tiny strings of frosted crystal beads and set it next to the crèche. There it stood guardian over the manger scene we had used ever since our first Christmas as newlyweds.

Our intention was to use this little version of our old tree until our daughter had her own home, and then give it to her to begin her own Christmas traditions with a bit of the tree she had enjoyed from babyhood.

The day our daughter arrived for Christmas break, we held our breath as she rushed into the house eager to place her special ornaments on the tree. She stopped in front of the new tree, looked at it critically for a few moments, and then turned with a perplexed frown.

"You got a new tree!" she said, a trace of disappointment in her voice.

"Do you like it?" I asked.

She studied it for a few moments, touched the boughs, and traced her finger along the curves of red garland draped around the tree. "It's prettier, and bigger, but I guess it's just not the same. You know, our tradition."

"Not to worry," her father said, beaming. "Check this out!" He pointed proudly at the smaller version of Bartholomew standing guard over the Holy Family. "Now you can start your own tradition!"

"Oh, Dad," she laughed, throwing her arms around her father's neck. "You know me too well! I love it!"

I think I saw the gleam of a tear in her eyes as she kissed her father and realized that traditions are not so much rooted in things, but in the love that gives them meaning. And as long as that love remains, changing our traditions will never ruin Christmas.

Pamela Kennedy is a freelance writer of short stories, articles, essays, and children's books. Wife of a retired naval officer and mother of three children, she has made her home on both U.S. coasts and currently resides in Honolulu, Hawaii.

Original artwork by Doris Ettlinger.

Christmas Cards

Louise Dale Nelson

When the holidays are over,
And I have some time to spare,
I gather all the Christmas cards
And find an easy chair.
I pull up closer to the fire,
Take time to reminisce,
I read again each line and verse,
Lest something I might miss.

I try to pick the prettiest,
But I can't decide.
The ones I think on longest
Contain messages inside.
There between the pages
Is a special bit of news
About the crops or weather,
Or when the baby's due.

"I can't explain the way I feel,"
Says a friend as pure as gold.
But the simple words, "We love you,"
Make our blessings manifold.
The postman living here receives
A special one of beauty,
"Thanks for all the little things,"
Beyond his call of duty.

Oh, yes! The ones with pictures
We cherish most of all;
It's amazing how the children
Have grown to be so tall.
We sign cards with our heartstrings
And send them out to share
Our love and hopes for "Peace on Earth"
To people everywhere.

When we hear old, beloved carols
And crystal stars wink from the tree,
We read each card and old friends smile
From the corners of our memory.

—HELEN DARBY BERNING

*A collage of old-fashioned Christmas cards
brings back warm memories. Photograph by Jessie Walker.*

COUNTRY CHRONICLE

Lansing Christman

WINTER BIRTHDAY THOUGHTS

This December marks my ninety-fifth birthday. In the many winters of my past, I have learned that a bright beacon of hope is always there—the winter sunshine. That beam of sunlight paves a protected path through this occasionally forbidding season and makes it easier for me to accommodate the ice and snow.

In winter evenings, other things ease me through the long hours. Outside, in the soothing quiet of the still, crisp air, the gleaming stars and the glowing moon pierce the shadowy, snow-covered hillsides and create their own severe beauty. They seem to be reminding me that the riotous colors of other seasons are not the only treasures of nature.

Inside, I enjoy the long, slow evenings by the fire reading my favorite books and reacquainting myself with old friends. The elderly calico curls up in one soft circle of pleasure beside my feet; stretched comfortably on the fireplace rug is the newest resident, the orange tabby who adopted this place last summer.

Perhaps a symphony or an opera will bring the exquisite joys of imagination to my evening hours. Songs of honor and love, courage and tragedy take me out of the confines of this cozy room.

I may also recall the winters of my childhood, when we sledded down nearby hills or skated on the farm pond. The laughter and the voices of brothers and sisters and cousins and friends still echo in my thoughts and make me smile.

Yes, with a few days of sunshine in the weeks ahead I will be content. The gentle touch of the sun's warmth will reach down from the bright blue skies, carry tomorrow's promise, and lessen the power of the storms that are yet to come. The days will begin to lengthen and bring with them a gratifying assurance of the cyclical motion of life itself. I know, after ninety-five years, that there is always a spring to come.

The author of four books, Lansing Christman has contributed to IDEALS *for more than thirty years. He lives in rural South Carolina.*

A comfortable chair and a warm fire are an invitation to enjoy a quiet holiday moment. Photograph by Jessie Walker.

83

New Year's Eve

Alfred, Lord Tennyson

Ring out, wild bells, to the wild sky,
The flying cloud, the frosty light;
The year is dying in the night.
Ring out, wild bells, and let him die.

Ring out the old, ring in the new;
Ring, happy bells, across the snow;
The year is going, let him go.
Ring out the false, ring in the true.

Ring out the grief that saps the mind,
For those we see no more;
Ring out the feud of rich and poor;
Ring in redress to all mankind.

Ring out a slowly dying cause,
And ancient forms of party strife;

Ring in the nobler modes of life,
With sweeter manners, purer laws.

Ring out false pride in place and blood,
The civic slander and the spite;
Ring in the love of truth and right;
Ring in the common love of good.

Ring out old shapes of foul disease,
Ring out the narrowing lust of gold,
Ring out the thousand wars of old,
Ring in the thousand years of peace.

Ring in the valiant man and free,
The larger heart, the kindlier hand.
Ring out the darkness of the land;
Ring in the Christ that is to be.

*The sun highlighting the snow makes a winter day
beautiful in Cleveland National Forest, California.
Photograph by Christopher Talbot Frank.*

READERS' FORUM

Snapshots from our IDEALS readers

Left: "Catch me if you can!" Three-year-old Sarah Agnes Stolt, daughter of Dana Brown and Mark Stolt of Rhode Island, is eager to sample her mother's gingerbread men. Ann Stolt, of Rockville, Maryland, is very proud of her great-niece.

Below: Seven-month-old Caden Tuson, son of Brett and Laura Tuson of Bellevue, Washington, is delighted with his first Christmas celebration. His grandfather, Rex Kennedy, is very proud of his first grandchild, who was born on his birthday.

Left: "Where are the reindeer?" Noah Huffaker is ready to take over Santa's duties. In the meantime he is wearing his grandfather's hat and supervising his grandparents, Dennis and Pam Greer of Garden Grove, California, as they complete holiday preparations.

Below left: Mason Carroccio, son of Shawn and Heather Carroccio, of Findlay, Ohio, is fascinated with his cousin Tyler Kline's new Christmas decoration. Tyler's parents are Kyle and Ammie Kline of Marysville, Ohio. Great-Grandmother Shirley Kline, of Mount Cory, Ohio, shared this photograph with IDEALS.

THANK YOU for sharing your family photographs with IDEALS. We hope to hear from other readers who would like to share snapshots with the IDEALS family. Please include a self-addressed, stamped envelope if you would like the photos returned; or keep your original photographs for safekeeping and send duplicate photos along with your name, address, and telephone number to:

Readers' Forum
Ideals Publications
535 Metroplex Drive, Suite 250
Nashville, Tennessee 37211

Publisher, Patricia A. Pingry
Editor, Marjorie Lloyd
Designer, Marisa Calvin
Copy Editor, Melinda Rathjen
Permissions Editor, Patsy Jay
Contributing Writers, Michelle Prater Burke,
Lansing Christman, Maud Dawson, Joan Donaldson,
Pamela Kennedy, Melissa Lester, Lois Winston

ACKNOWLEDGMENTS

BENNETT, DEBORAH, A. "Reverie" from Mature Years, Winter 2001. Submitted for use in Ideals by the author. CROWELL, GRACE, NOLL. "Let Us Keep Christmas." Previously used in Ideals Christmas, 1944, by permission of the author. Used here by permission of Claire Cumberworth. JAQUES, EDNA. "Snowstorm" from Roses in December. Published by Thomas Allen Ltd., 1952. Used by permission of Louise Bonnell. TROTT, ROSEMARY CLIFFORD. "To a New House At Christmas," Previously published in Good Housekeeping. Submitted for use in Ideals by the author. Our sincere thanks to Thomas P. Carrol for "The Star." Previously used in Ideals Christmas, 1944, by special permission of The Atlantian. Our sincere thanks to those authors, or their heirs, some of whom we were unable to locate, who submitted poems or articles to Ideals for publication. Every possible effort has been made to acknowledge ownership of material used.

Left: Two-year-old Brandon Lee Sarrett welcomes young Payton Luanne to the family. Terry and Luanne Stanley of Kimberly, West Virginia, told IDEALS that "grandchildren are such a blessing."